SUPER SPORTS STAR
VINCE CARTER

Stew Thornley

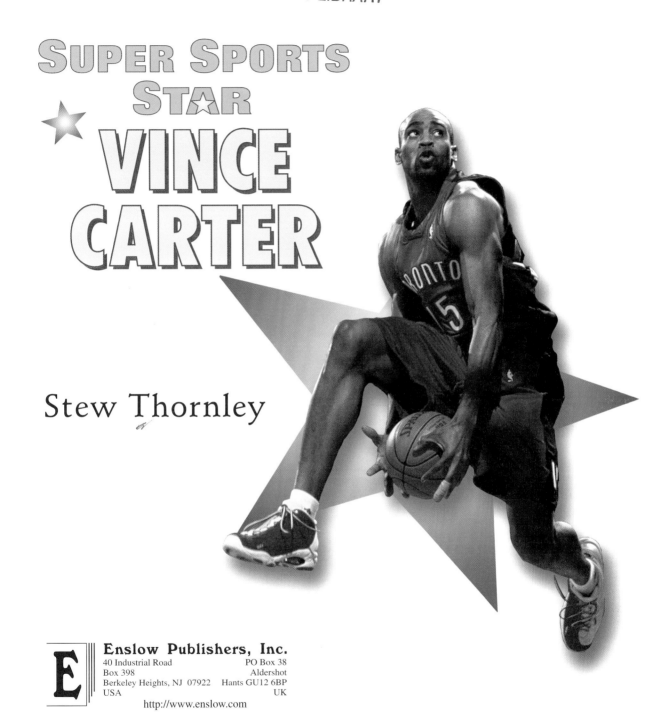

E ‖ **Enslow Publishers, Inc.**

40 Industrial Road   PO Box 38
Box 398   Aldershot
Berkeley Heights, NJ 07922 Hants GU12 6BP
USA   UK

http://www.enslow.com

Library of Congress Cataloging-in-Publication Data

Thornley, Stew.
 Super sports star Vince Carter / Stew Thornley.
    p. cm. — (Super sports star)
Includes bibliographical references (p.   ) and index.
 ISBN 0-7660-1805-9
1. Carter, Vince—Juvenile literature. 2. Basketball players—United States—Biography—Juvenile literature. [1. Carter, Vince. 2. Basketball players. 3. African Americans—Biography.] I. Title. II. Series.
  GV884.C39 T56   2002
  796.323'092—dc21

                                        2001000813

Printed in the United States of America

10 9 8 7 6 5 4 3 2 1

To Our Readers: We have done our best to make sure all Internet addresses in this book were active and appropriate when we went to press. However, the author and the publisher have no control over and assume no liability for the material available on those Internet sites or on other Web sites they may link to. Any comments or suggestions can be sent by e-mail to comments@enslow.com or to the address on the back cover.

Photo Credits: Andy Hayt/NBA Photos, pp. 9, 26; Bill Baptist/NBA Photos, p. 6; Fernando Medina/NBA Photos, pp. 8, 16, 31, 33, 40; Frank McGrath/NBA Photos, p. 10; Garrett Ellwood/NBA Photos, pp. 1, 44; Glenn James/NBA Photos, pp. 4, 29, 38; Jerry Wachter/NBA Photos, p. 20; Nathaniel S. Butler/NBA Photos, p. 18; Noren Trotman/NBA Photos, pp. 11, 14, 24, 36; Rocky Widner/NBA Photos, p. 22.

Cover Photo: Garrett Ellwood/NBA Photos

CONTENTS

Introduction

Vince Carter is not a huge man, but he plays basketball like a giant. Carter plays at the guard and forward positions for the Toronto Raptors of the National Basketball Association (NBA). He is six feet seven inches tall and he can jump high in the air to grab rebounds away from taller players.

On the ground, he can dribble and pass the ball. He can play defense, and he can also score points. He can connect on an outside shot, far away from the basket. But those things are not what really thrill the fans. They love to see him dunk the ball.

Carter's dunks often make the highlight shows. Opposing players hate it when they end up in those highlights. It means Carter dunked over them. When he was in college, Carter started keeping a list of players he dunked over. He kept the list going when he got to the NBA. Today, the list includes great players like Alonzo Mourning, Dikembe Mutombo, and Patrick Ewing.

Vince Carter is great at dunk shots, but he wants to be known for more than just dunking the ball. "Dunkers come and go," he says. "You can go to the playground and find a bunch of guys who can do fancy dunks. The great players excel at all aspects of the game. That's what I want to be."

CHAPTER 1

Achieving Greatness

Vince Carter was on fire when he won the NBA Slam-Dunk Contest in February 2000. The next day he played in the All-Star Game. He had more exciting plays in that contest as well.

Near the end of February, the Raptors played the Phoenix Suns. The game was on national television and Carter scored 25 points in the first half. He stayed hot in the third quarter. The Raptors led by two points when Carter took a bounce pass from Charles Oakley. Carter got set as if he were going to shoot, but instead he drove toward the baseline.

He raced by Luc Longley of the Suns. Penny Hardaway also tried to block his path, but Carter spun to his right. When he was in the air, he whirled completely around. He shot the ball, and it dropped through the basket. Carter was also fouled on the play. He stepped to the free-throw line and made his shot to give Toronto a 60–55 lead.

Phoenix scored to close the gap. When the Raptors came back down the court, Tracy McGrady had the ball. He drove in for the shot, but Jason Kidd blocked it. The ball sailed high into the air, and Vince Carter swooped in from the other side. He leaped high. With the ball still above the rim, he got his hand on it. He slammed it home.

The Suns fought back and led in the final quarter, but Carter changed that. He hit three straight jump shots to put the Raptors back in the lead. Going into the final minute of the game, the Raptors were ahead by two points. Carter took a pass in the left corner of the court.

Vince Carter seems to fly through the air as he glides toward the basket.

Jason Kidd and Tom Gugliotta covered him. Carter was double-teamed, but he broke away from both defenders. Then Carter lost control of the ball. But he reached down, picked it up, and made the shot. The basket gave him 51 points in the game. Toronto went on to win, 103–102.

That was the most points Carter had ever

scored in a professional game. "I've never had 50 before. Not in high school, or college. I think I had 55 one summer league against a bunch of kids but never in a real game."

There was another player who could excite the fans like Carter. His name was Michael Jordan. Now Carter was being compared to Jordan. Both had played college basketball at North Carolina. Both could make spectacular dunks. Both could have great games like Carter had just had. But Carter does not want to be the next Michael Jordan. He just wants to be the first Vince Carter.

Vince Carter soars past his defenders on his way **toward the basket.**

CHAPTER 2

Basketball Crazy

Vince Carter has always loved playing basketball. When he was six years old, he already knew he wanted to be a professional basketball player. His family helped him to achieve that goal. They all believed in him.

Growing up, Vince Carter was involved in many things, including sports.

When he played, Carter made believe he was Julius Erving. Erving was a great star in the NBA who was known for his exciting dunks. Before long, Carter would be known for the same thing. Carter could already dunk a basketball by the time he was in seventh grade. He was five feet eight inches tall at that time. That is not usually tall enough to dunk, but not many people could jump like Carter.

Vince Carter was born on January 26, 1977, in Daytona Beach, Florida. He also grew up in Daytona Beach. His mother, Michelle Carter-Robinson, and stepfather were both teachers. Carter's stepfather, Harry Robinson, entered Vince Carter's life when Vince was seven.

Vince Carter's parents made sure he was involved in other things besides sports. They did the same with Carter's younger brother, Christopher. "We kept him very active," Carter's mother said of Vince. "I guess that's why he turned out to be such a good kid. We kept him busy, and he didn't have time to get into any trouble."

Vince Carter played the saxophone when he was young. Later he played in his high school marching band. Carter even helped write his school's homecoming song. Carter also was a drum major. His mom remembered, "One of my proudest moments was watching Vince lead the band."

Carter did many things well. He was a good student who had many different talents. But it was basketball that made him stand out. He learned how to play at the YMCA in Daytona Beach. Dick Toth taught him many lessons. Toth was also the athletics director at Mainland High School, where Carter ended up a few years later.

Carter also did well in track and volleyball. In junior high, he was quarterback on the football team. Basketball was his best sport though. At Mainland High, Carter was the star of the team. He was a great shooter. Fans loved to watch him play. They were really amazed by how high he could jump.

Carter became known as "U. F. O."—unidentified flying object. He was also an incredible flying object. Vince Carter also became known outside of Florida. In 1995, he was picked to play on the 1995 USA Basketball

In high school, Carter became known as a "U.F.O."—unidentified flying object—for his great leaping ability.

Junior Team. He also made the High School All-America Team. Vince Carter was one of the best high-school players in the country.

Carter was a great, young basketball player, but he was also a good person. Charles Brinkerhoff was Carter's coach at Mainland High School. Brinkerhoff later said, "Vince is a lot more than the best player I've ever had. His influence on youngsters in this town is terrific. He's also a good friend. As a person, he's one in a million."

★★★ UP CLOSE

When Vince Carter outgrew his clothing, even things he never wore, his mom remembers her son giving them to school friends. And during those nights when Carter's parents took the family out for dinner, Vince Carter would invite his friends.

A Terrific Tar Heel

Many colleges offered scholarships—money to pay for college—to Carter. Most schools wanted him to play basketball. Carter decided to go to the University of North Carolina to play basketball and get an education.

A lot of basketball players who go to college do not always finish all four years of their education. Many of the best college players go directly to the NBA after just a few years of college. Carter's mother wanted to make sure that Vince would someday graduate. She made him sign an agreement. It said he would finish his studies and get his degree even if he left college early to play in the NBA.

At North Carolina, Carter focused his studies on African-American history. He also played basketball. Carter became friendly with another new player, Antawn Jamison. Jamison was a forward on the team. The North Carolina Tar Heels did not have many good forwards, so Jamison got to play right away.

Carter was not so lucky. The Tar Heels already had a good backcourt. That meant that Carter, as a guard, did not play much during his first year.

He got to play more in his second year of college, as a sophomore. In 1996–97, Carter shared the backcourt with Shammond Williams and Ed Cota. In the frontcourt, the Tar Heels had Jamison, Serge Zwikker, and Ademola Okulaja. It was an outstanding team. North Carolina also had an outstanding coach. Dean Smith was in his thirty-sixth season as coach at North Carolina. The Tar Heels had won two national championships with his help. Smith

Carter's mother made him promise that he would finish college and get his degree, even if he left college early to play in the NBA.

thought this team had a chance to win another title.

When the season opened, the Tar Heels struggled. They lost their first three games. Then they got hot, and won twelve straight games. That put them in the NCAA Tournament, the national college tournament.

North Carolina won its first three games. A win over Louisville would put the Tar Heels in the Final Four, the final round of games among the four teams in the NCAA Tournament. The Tar Heels built a big lead, but Louisville fought back. North Carolina led, 69–66. Then Carter took an inbounds pass and streaked in for a lay-up. After Louisville missed a shot, Carter got the ball and was fouled. He made a free throw. Soon after, he made two more free throws. Thanks to Carter, North Carolina opened up a safe lead again. North Carolina went on to win the game.

The Tar Heels were now only two games away from the championship. They played the

Vince Carter perfected many of the skills he would take to the NBA as a college player at the University of North Carolina.

Arizona Wildcats in the semifinal game. The Tar Heels were awesome in the first five minutes, and Vince Carter was a big part of it. He passed to Zwikker, who sank a basket. Carter also slapped the ball away from Arizona's Miles Simon. Jamison got the ball and fired a long pass. Carter took the pass on the run and headed for the basket. He made a lay-up and was fouled. Soon after, Cota threw an alley-oop pass. Carter grabbed it and slammed it through the basket. The Tar Heels had a 15–6 lead.

Arizona came back and closed the gap. Then Carter went to work again.

He and Cota combined on

another alley-oop basket. Carter then took a pass from Jamison. With his back to the basket, he jumped and dunked the ball behind his head. Later, he grabbed a loose ball and drove in for a lay-up. Carter had 15 points in the first half.

Miles Simon also had 15 points in the half, and Arizona came back to lead by three at halftime. Arizona won the game, 66–58, but Carter led North Carolina with 21 points.

His performance topped off a good season. Carter did even better during his third year, as a junior.

He had worked on his shooting over the off-season and the practice paid off. During the season, Carter made nearly 60 percent of his shots. Many were dunks. Others were outside shots. Carter increased his scoring average to 15.6 points per game. He also averaged 5.1 rebounds. Those are good totals for a guard. Carter also played excellent defense.

The Tar Heels ended up in the Final Four again.

Vince Carter worked on his shooting skills during his time at the University of North Carolina.

In the semifinal game, Carter scored 21 points—the most scored by any player on either team. However, North Carolina lost to Utah. For the second year in a row, the Tar Heels had been knocked out in the semifinal game.

It would not be easy for North Carolina to get back to the Final Four the next year. Antawn Jamison announced he was leaving college early. He would be entering the NBA. Vince Carter decided to do the same thing.

North Carolina would be hurt by the loss of these two stars. But Jamison and Carter were both ready to take their game to the next level.

CHAPTER 4

Turning Pro

The NBA draft is the way that professional basketball teams pick new players each year. It is an exciting time for the top college players. A player will finally learn which NBA team he will be playing for. But sometimes there are surprises. For Vince Carter, this was one of those times.

Antawn Jamison was the fourth player chosen in the draft. The Toronto Raptors picked him. Carter was excited for his friend and college teammate. But then Carter got some excitement of his own. The Golden State Warriors had the next pick, and they chose Carter. Jamison and Carter had been selected one right after the other. But there was more to come.

The Raptors and Warriors exchanged players. Jamison and Carter were swapped for one another. That meant Carter would be playing for Toronto and Jamison would go to the Golden State Warriors.

The Raptors were a new team. They had

After the Golden State Warriors and Toronto Raptors swapped players, Vince Carter became a member of the Raptors.

NBA.com
Slam Dunk Champion
Saturday, February 12

been in the league for only three seasons. Toronto had won only sixteen games the year before. The Raptors were working hard to become a better team. They knew Carter would help them do that.

Glen Grunwald, Toronto's general manager, knew Vince Carter was a good player and a good person. Team officials in Toronto were impressed with Carter's basketball ability and the strength of his beliefs.

Carter was eager to start his NBA career, but he had to wait. There was a disagreement between the players and the owners, and the season got started very late.

Carter finally got the chance to play his first game on February 5, 1999. He had 16 points, as the Raptors beat Boston. It was a good start.

Carter's games were not always great in his first month. He had a bad shooting game at Detroit. But he came back the next night and scored 28 points.

Carter picked up steam in March. Against

Atlanta, he made several baskets on alley-oop passes. He also made an over-the-head dunk in the face of Dikembe Mutombo. This was great stuff. Carter liked being spectacular. He also liked winning. He thought the two went together. "Anytime I can get a highlight play, I will," Carter said. "It motivates the team."

With Carter leading the way, the Raptors won 11 of their 17 games in March. One of the wins, by two points, was against Detroit. Carter scored 17 points in the final quarter of that game. In a game near the end of the month, Toronto was tied with San Antonio. There were 17 seconds left. During a time-out, the Raptors huddled and planned a play. Coach Butch Carter said, "Get it to Vince, and he'll win the game for us."

Vince Carter did just that. Carter had worked hard to learn to be a great player. He still asked his parents for advice. "After every game, I call them and get their take on how I've played," he said. "They've been there from

Vince Carter struggles to hold onto the ball and keep his balance.

Day 1." Carter also learned from some of the Raptors' older players, especially Charles Oakley.

It was a great year for Carter and the Raptors. The team did not make the playoffs, but it improved its record. Vince Carter was named the NBA's Rookie of the Year.

After the final game of the season, Carter threw his shoes and sweatbands into the stands. It was his way of thanking the Toronto fans for their support. He also promised them that the Raptors would make the playoffs the next year.

Of course, Carter had another promise he had to keep. He had to finish college like he had promised his mother he would.

Dazzling Dunks

During the summer in 1999, Vince Carter returned to college. He took classes in computers, communications, and African-American history. He was working toward graduating.

In January 2000, Carter had a great game against Milwaukee. He scored 47 points. It was the most points ever scored by a Toronto player. He broke the old team record when he hit a three-point shot early in the third quarter. He followed that up with a thundering dunk. He then played tough defense down the stretch. The Raptors won, 115–110.

Carter was doing it all. But it was still the dunks that were making him stand out. He had become one of the league's most popular players. The fans vote for the players in the All-Star Game. Carter received more votes than any other player in the NBA. In fact, he had the second-highest vote total ever. Only Michael Jordan had ever received more votes.

The day before the All-Star Game, Carter

Vince Carter's only defender is beaten as Carter takes off for the basket.

had another job. He took part in the slam-dunk contest. The fans expected Carter to put on a great show. For his first dunk, he slowly dribbled in. Then he jumped and spun to his right. In the air, he turned all the way around. He swung his right arm, with the ball in it. With a windmill motion, he dunked the ball. He received a perfect score of 50 for the dunk.

On another dunk, Carter started without the ball. Teammate Tracy McGrady had it near the free-throw line. As Carter came in, McGrady bounced the ball off the floor. Carter caught it and leaped toward the basket. He took the ball in his left hand and passed it between his legs to his right hand. He then slammed the ball through the basket. But he was not done yet. Carter stared up at the basket and posed. It was all part of the show.

The fans loved it and the other All-Stars enjoyed it, too. Shaquille O'Neal stood with a video camera. His mouth dropped open in amazement. Other players stared in disbelief. Carter went on to win the slam-dunk event.

The next day was the All-Star Game, and Carter kept up the highlights. He finished the game with 12 points and 4 rebounds.

Even when he was surrounded by All-Stars, Vince Carter stood out.

CHAPTER 6
Helping the Raptors

Playing in the All-Star Game had been fun. But Vince Carter wanted to help the Raptors win. On February 21, he helped the Raptors battle back. They trailed the New York Knicks by 10 points early in the second half. But then Carter rattled off 11 straight points. Toronto went on to a 99–88 win.

The next week, Carter had his 51-point game against Phoenix. But for Carter, the fun was just starting.

On March 2, the Raptors played the Boston Celtics. The game was close. Boston led by two points with 3.2 seconds left. Carter took the inbounds pass. He dribbled three times and fired. It was a fadeaway shot from beyond the three-point line. As the buzzer sounded to end the game, the ball fell through the hoop. Carter's shot won the game, 97–96, for Toronto.

Seven days later, Carter did it again. The Raptors and Los Angeles Clippers battled down to the wire. Carter had tied the game with a

Vince Carter **s t r e t c h e s** out over his defender as he tries to make a shot.

long jump shot with 51 seconds to play. But the Clippers went ahead, 94–92, with 1.5 seconds left. Toronto called a timeout. They then inbounded the ball at midcourt. Tracy McGrady got the ball to Carter. He fired a three-point attempt. It fell through the basket as time ran out. Once again, the Raptors had a last-minute win, thanks to Carter.

In mid-March, Carter went for the dunk to win a game. The Raptors and Houston Rockets were tied. Carter took the ball with 11 seconds left in the game. He stood at the baseline to let time run down. Finally, he shot toward the basket. Shandon Anderson tried to stop him, but it did not work. Carter raced by and dunked the ball, and the Raptors won again.

Toronto had the fourth-best record in the Eastern Conference. The top eight teams in each conference make it to the playoffs. The Raptors slowed down a bit over the final month of the regular season. But they still made the playoffs for the first time in their history.

Vince Carter stretches out his arm to try to block the shot.

Vince Carter had a great season. He averaged 25.5 points per game. That was the fourth-best scoring average in the league. Unfortunately, the Raptors did not last long in the playoffs. They were beaten by the New York Knicks, who won every game. But the Raptors had improved. And Vince Carter had kept his promise to the fans to get the Raptors to the playoffs.

He kept working on his promise to his mom, too. Once again, he studied so that he could get his college degree.

It would be a busy summer. Besides his studies, Carter looked forward to a new challenge. He was a member of the 2000 United States Olympic Basketball Team. He and his teammates won a gold medal.

★★★ **UP CLOSE**

Vince Carter likes playing video games. He also plays golf and backgammon. He still plays the saxophone. He also loves meeting people.

In the summer of 2001, Vince Carter raised money for different charities. Vince Carter is a big star now, but he is still the same person he was before he became famous. Friends say he has not changed.

CAREER STATISTICS

College							
Team	**Year**	**GP**	**FG%**	**FT%**	**Reb.**	**Ast.**	**PPG**
North Carolina	1995–96	31	.492	.689	119	40	7.5
North Carolina	1996–97	34	.525	.750	152	83	13.0
North Carolina	1997–98	38	.591	.680	195	74	15.6
Totals		**103**	**.547**	**.705**	**466**	**197**	**12.3**

NBA									
Team	**Year**	**GP**	**FG%**	**FT%**	**Reb.**	**Ast.**	**Stl.**	**Blk.**	**PPG**
Toronto	1998–99	50	.450	.761	283	149	55	77	18.3
Toronto	1999–2000	82	.465	.791	476	322	110	92	25.7
Totals		**132**	**.460**	**.781**	**759**	**471**	**165**	**169**	**22.9**

GP—Games Played   **Reb.**—Rebounds   **Blk.**—Blocked Shots
FG%—Field Goal Percentage   **Ast.**—Assists   **Pts.**—Points
FT%—Free Throw Percentage   **Stl.**—Steals   **PPG**—Points Per Game

Where to Write to Vince Carter

Mr. Vince Carter
Toronto Raptors
Air Canada Centre
40 Bay Street
Toronto, Ontario M5J 2X2

WORDS TO KNOW

alley-oop—A pass thrown toward the basket so that a teammate can take the pass in the air and dunk the ball.

assist—A pass to a teammate who makes a basket.

backcourt—The half of the court farthest from the basket a team is shooting at. The backcourt also refers to a team's guards.

bank shot—A shot that bounces (or banks) off the backboard.

baseline—The out-of-bounds line that runs behind the basket.

double-teaming—Two defenders on a player.

draft—The way that NBA teams pick new players each year.

dunk—A shot that is slammed through the basket from directly above the basket. Also known as a slam or slam dunk.

Final Four—The final games, among four teams, in the NCAA Tournament.

freshman—A first-year student in college or high school.

jump hook—A one-handed shot taken while jumping.

jump shot—A shot taken while jumping.

junior—A third-year student in college or high school.

NCAA Tournament—The national college tournament. NCAA stands for National Collegiate Athletic Association.

outside shot—A shot far away from the basket.

rebound—Getting the ball after a missed shot.

senior—A student in his or her last year of college or high school.

sophomore—A second-year student in college or high school.

triple-teaming—Putting three defenders on a player.

turnaround—A shot taken after the player has turned to face the basket.

READING ABOUT

Harris, Bill. *Vince Carter: Air Canada*. Champaign, Il.: Sports Publishing, Inc., 1999.

Smith, Doug. *The Vince Carter Story*. New York, N.Y.: Scholastic, Inc., 2001.

Stewart, Mark. *Vince Carter: The Fire Burns Bright*. Brookfield, Conn.: Millbrook Press, Inc., 2001.

Internet Addresses

The Official Web Site of the NBA
    <http://www.nba.com/playerfile/vince_carter.html>

Sporting News Draft Profile: Vince Carter
    <http://www.sportingnews.com/nba/draft/profiles/carter.html>

INDEX